THE GREAT SCIENTISTS

Albert Einstein

Kavita Sharma and Aaliya Roy Kundal

Om Books International

Wish you could time travel? Go back in time to hunt with the cavemen or rush to the future a hundred years from now? Do you think it is even possible? Well, one of the world's most famous scientists thought you can! His name: Albert Einstein.

Albert Einstein was born on 14 March 1879, in Ulm, a small city in Germany. Einstein was born a healthy baby, but with a big head. His mother, Pauline Koch, was worried about

the shape of his head. Little did she know about all the wonderful ideas that would emerge from his amazing head later. His head, of course, became the right size just a few weeks after his birth.

Soon after his birth, Einstein's family moved to Munich, a bigger city in Germany. There he began school when he was six years old. Einstein was not happy at school, but loved music, mathematics and physics. His father, Hermann Einstein, had an electrical business, and little Einstein spent a lot of time there learning about mathematics and physics. Another of his favourite things was playing with a compass and making card decks.

When Einstein finished school, he joined the Swiss Federal Polytechnic Institute in Zurich, Switzerland. He passed out with a diploma to teach physics but could not get a teaching job. One day, Einstein was offered the job of a clerk at the Swiss Patent

Office in Bern. He took that job. There he spent time studying other people's inventions and working on his own scientific ideas. In 1903, Einstein married Mileva Maric and they had two sons, Hans Albert and Eduard.

The miracle years of the genius scientist Einstein began in 1905. He made many important discoveries in the world of physics about light, energy, gravity, space, and time.

But Einstein is most well known for his 'theory of relativity' and the equation $e=mc^2$, which proves that even the smallest amount of mass (basically the amount of stuff anything is made of) can be turned into a lot of energy. And that energy too can be converted into mass! Now that's some discovery, and it made Einstein very famous!

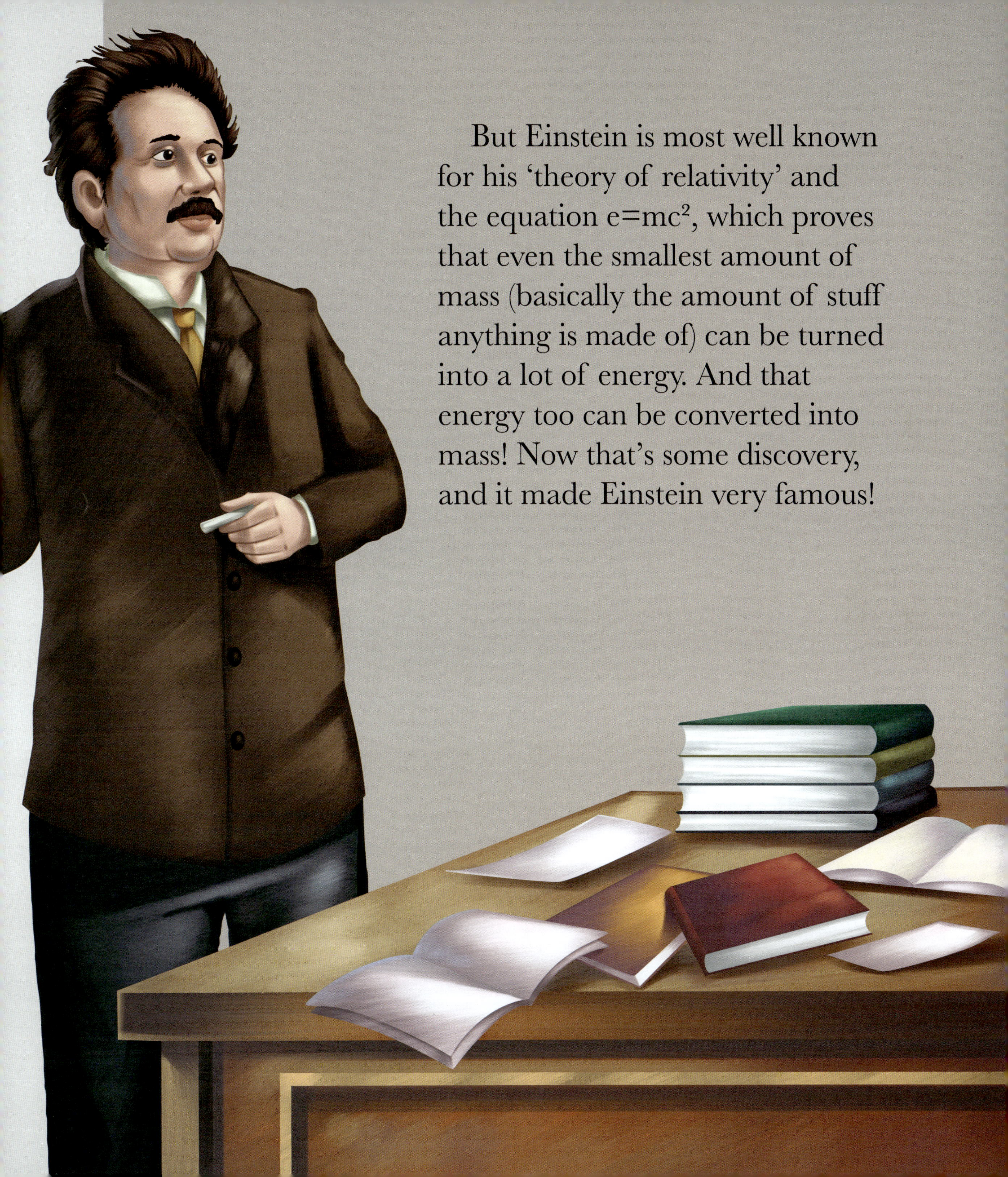

Einstein was also a great teacher. He first began teaching as a professor of physics at the University of Zurich. People at the university thought he was rather funny. He forgot to wear his socks and rarely combed his hair. His students loved him!

Around the year 1914, things were getting bad across Europe. World War I was just starting. Einstein was a believer in peace and hated the war. Even in the time of war, he continued to work on his scientific theories. In 1921, Einstein won the prestigious Nobel Prize for Physics for his work on the behaviour of light.

Although Einstein was happy about his work, things were becoming tough for the Jewish people in Germany, Einstein's home. Einstein himself was a Jew and did not like how Jews were being treated in Germany. In December 1932, Einstein moved to America and began teaching at the Institute for Advanced Study in Princeton.

Around the early 1940s, Einstein's famous equation $e=mc^2$ is said to have been the basis for creating the world's most dangerous weapon – the atom bomb. Einstein was a lover of peace and did not himself contribute to creating the bomb. At the end of the World War II in 1945, he was horrified by the destruction caused by the use of the atom bomb.

Einstein spoke against it and fought for peace till he died on 18 April 1955, at the age of 76.

Scandium
Tantalum
6x6
100dollars
light
benzol
123

1/2 v²/c²
x = XO(1-[
/(c²
(c+V)
(c+V)
K = ∫F d
MkBT

After Einstein died, Thomas Harvey, the doctor who examined his body, discovered that the mathematical thinking part of Einstein's brain was 15 per cent larger than normal!

Einstein did many incredible things in his life. He gave the world some of the most powerful scientific theories. He inspired people to dream of impossible things. That is why in 1999, the Time magazine called him 'Person of the Century'. Albert Einstein was a true genius!

So coming back to time travel…

You know that nothing in this universe travels faster than light, right? Einstein discovered that if a person is able to travel at a speed close to the speed of light, time will slow down for him. So if you spend 5 years on a spaceship that travelled at the speed of light, only 5 years will pass for you on the spaceship, but on earth as many as 50 years would have passed. So when you come back to Earth, your friends would have grown old and your teachers would have retired. You would then have travelled ahead in time to the future!